Smart Air Fryer Recipes

Easy, Delicious and Affordable Air Fryer Recipes for a Healthy Lifestyle

Linda Wang

© **Copyright 2021 by Linda Wang - All rights reserved.**

The content contained within this book may not be reproduced, duplicated or transmitted without direct written permission from the author or the publisher.
Under no circumstances will any blame or legal responsibility be held against the publisher, or author, for any damages, reparation, or monetary loss due to the information contained within this book. Either directly or indirectly.

Legal Notice:
This book is copyright protected. This book is only for personal use. You cannot amend, distribute, sell, use, quote or paraphrase any part, or the content within this book, without the consent of the author or publisher.

Disclaimer Notice:
Please note the information contained within this document is for educational and entertainment purposes only. All effort has been executed to present accurate, up to date, and reliable, complete information. No warranties of any kind are declared or implied. Readers acknowledge that the author is not engaging in the rendering of legal, financial, medical or professional advice. The content within this book has been derived from various sources. Please consult a licensed professional before attempting any techniques outlined in this book.
By reading this document, the reader agrees that under no circumstances is the author responsible for any losses, direct or indirect, which are incurred as a result of the use of information contained within this document, including, but not limited to, — errors, omissions, or inaccuracies.

TABLE OF CONTENTS

INTRODUCTION 1

Healthy Squash 5

Strasbourg Potatoes and Sausages with Curry 7

Sausage Solo 9

Toad-in-the-Hole Tarts 11

Ham and Cheese Patties 13

Herbed Omelet 14

Tofu and Bell Peppers 16

Cumin Eggplant Mix 17

Broccoli Stew 19

Cheese and Macaroni Balls 20

Mozzarella Patties 22

Green Bean Casserole 24

Cabbage and Radishes Mix 26

Coriander Artichokes 28

Roasted Garlic 30

Kernel and Sweet Corn Fritters 32

Easy Sweet Potato Curry Fries 34

Swordfish Steaks and Tomatoes 35

Salmon Jerky 37

Lime Baked Salmon 39

Salmon and Jasmine Rice 41

Chicken with Pineapple 42

Chicken Curry 44

Chicken and Veggies 46

Turkey Meatballs 48

Paprika Lamb Chops 50

Chinese Style Pork Meatballs 52

Italian Beef Meatballs 54

Beef, Olives and Tomatoes 56

Sage Pork 57

Pork Sausage Casserole 59

Sautéed Pork with Peppers 61

Spicy Tofu 63

Spicy Mushroom Soup 65

Creamy Potato Soup 67

Air fryer Fish Stew 69

Avocado Bites 71

Crustless Pizza 73

Portabella Pizza Treat 75

Chicken Stuffed Mushrooms 77

Cocoa and Nuts Bombs 79

Tangy Mango Slices 81

Avocado and Raspberries Cake 83

Currant Pudding 85

Yummy Rice Pudding 87

Raisin Bread Pudding 89

Mouth-Watering Strawberry Cobbler 91

Sweet Potato Pie 93

Milky Doughnuts 96

Fruity Tacos 99

NOTES 101

INTRODUCTION

An Air Fryer is a magic revolutionized kitchen appliance that helps you fry with less or even no oil at all. This kind of product applies Rapid Air technology, which offers a new way to fry with less oil. This new invention cooks food through the circulation of superheated air and generates 80% low-fat food. Although the food is fried with less oil, you don't need to worry as the food processed by the Air Fryer still has the same taste like the food fried using the deep-frying method.

This technology uses a superheated element, which radiates heat close to the food and an exhaust fan in its lid to circulate airflow. An Air Fryer ensures that the food processed is cooked completely. The exhaust fan located at the top of the cooking chamber helps the food get the same heating temperature in every part quickly, resulting in a cooked food of better and healthier quality. Besides, cooking with an Air Fryer is also suitable for those individuals which are too busy or do not have enough time. For example, an Air Fryer only needs half a spoonful of oil and takes 10 minutes to serve a medium bowl of crispy French fries.

In addition to serving healthier food, an Air Fryer also provides some other benefits to you. Since an Air Fryer helps you fry using less oil or without oil for some kind of food, it automatically reduces the fat and cholesterol content in food. Indeed, no one will refuse to enjoy fried food without worrying about the greasy and fat content. Having fried food with no guilt is one of the pleasures of life. Besides having low fat and cholesterol, you save some amount of money by consuming oil sparingly, which can be used for other needs. An Air Fryer also can reheat your food. Sometimes, when you have fried leftover and you reheat it, it will usually serve reheated greasy food with some addition of unhealthy reuse oil. Undoubtedly, the saturated fat in the fried food gets worse because of this process. An Air Fryer helps you reheat your food without being afraid of extra oils that the food may absorb. Fried bananas, fish and chips, nuggets, or even fried chicken can be reheated to become as warm and crispy as they were before by using an Air Fryer.

Some people may think that spending some amount of money to buy a fryer is wasteful. I dare to say that they are wrong because an Air Fryer is not only used to fry. It is a sophisticated multi-function appliance since it also helps you to roast chicken, make steak, grill fish, and even bake a cake. With a built-in air filter, an Air Fryer filters the air and saves your kitchen from smoke and grease.

An air Fryer is really a new innovative method of cooking. Grab it fast and welcome to a clean and healthy kitchen.

Healthy Squash

Preparation Time: 10 minutes

Cooking Time: 25 minutes

Serve: 4

Ingredients:

- 2 lbs yellow squash, cut into half-moons
- ¼ tsp pepper
- 1 tsp Italian seasoning
- 1 tbsp olive oil
- ¼ tsp salt

Directions:

1. Add all ingredients into the large bowl and toss well.
2. Preheat the air fryer to 400 °F.
3. Add squash mixture into the air fryer basket and cook for 10 minutes.
4. Shake basket and cook for another 10 minutes.
5. Shake once again and cook for 5 minutes more.

Nutrition:

Calories 70, Fat 4 g, Carbohydrates 7 g, Sugar 4 g, Protein 2 g, Cholesterol 1 mg

Strasbourg Potatoes and Sausages with Curry

Preparation time: 10-20 minutes;

Cooking time: 15-30 minutes;

Serve: 6

Ingredients:

- 3 Strasbourg sausages
- 750 g of fresh potatoes
- 2 small spoons of curry
- Salt to taste

Direction:

1. Peel the potatoes and cut them into cubes of approximately 1 cm per side. Put the Perl apples to soak in water, drain them and dry them well with a paper towel.
2. After spraying the air fryer with cooking spray, pour potatoes, salt.

3. Set the temperature to 150 °C and simmer the potatoes for 20 minutes.
4. Add the Strasbourg sausages cut into small pieces, curry, and cook for another 10 minutes.

Nutrition:

Calories 418.5, Fat 17.6 g, Carbohydrate 42.1 g, Sugars 2.1 g, Protein 18.0 g, Cholesterol 44.5 mg

Sausage Solo

Preparation Time: 5 minutes

Cooking Time: 22 minutes

Servings: 4

Ingredients:

- 4 cooked sausages, sliced
- 6 eggs
- 2 bread slices, cut into sticks
- ½ cup mozzarella cheese, grated
- ½ cup cream

Directions:

1. Preheat the Air fryer to 355 degrees F and grease 4 ramekins lightly.
2. Whisk together eggs and cream in a bowl and beat well.
3. Transfer the egg mixture into ramekins and arrange the bread sticks and sausage slices around the edges.

4. Top with mozzarella cheese evenly and place the ramekins in Air fryer basket.
5. Cook for about 22 minutes and dish out to serve warm.

Nutrition:

Calories: 180, Fat: 12.7g, Carbs: 3.9g, Sugar: 1.3g, Protein: 12.4g, Sodium: 251mg

Toad-in-the-Hole Tarts

Preparation Time: 5 minutes

Cooking Time: 25 minutes

Servings: 4

Ingredients:

- 4 eggs
- 4 tablespoons cheddar cheese, shredded
- 1 sheet frozen puff pastry, thawed and cut into 4 squares
- 4 tablespoons cooked ham, diced
- 2 tablespoons fresh chives, chopped
- 1 tablespoon olive oil

Directions:

1. Preheat the Air fryer to 400 degrees F and grease an Air fryer basket.
2. Place 2 pastry squares in the air fryer basket and cook for about 8 minutes.
3. Remove Air fryer basket from the Air fryer and press each square gently with a metal

tablespoon to form an indentation.

4. Place 1 tablespoon of ham and 1 tablespoon of cheddar cheese in each hole and top with 1 egg each.
5. Return Air fryer basket to Air fryer and cook for about 6 more minutes.
6. Remove tarts from the Air fryer basket and allow to cool.
7. Repeat with remaining pastry squares, cheese, ham, and eggs.
8. Dish out and garnish tarts with chives.

Nutrition:

Calories: 175, Fat: 13.7g, Carbohydrates: 4.1g, Sugar: 0.5g, Protein: 9.3g, Sodium: 233mg

Ham and Cheese Patties

Preparation Time: 20 minutes

Servings: 4

Ingredients:

- 8 ham slices; chopped.
- 4 handfuls mozzarella cheese; grated
- 1 puff pastry sheet
- 4 tsp. mustard

Directions:

1. Roll out puff pastry on a working surface and cut it in 12 squares. Divide cheese, ham and mustard on half of them, top with the other halves and seal the edges
2. Place all the patties in your air fryer's basket and cook at 370 °F for 10 minutes. Divide the patties between plates and serve

Herbed Omelet

Preparation Time: 20 minutes

Servings: 4

Ingredients:

- 6 eggs; whisked
- 2 tbsp. parmesan cheese; grated
- 4 tbsp. heavy cream
- 1 tbsp. parsley; chopped.

- 1 tbsp. tarragon; chopped.
- 2 tbsp. chives; chopped.
- Salt and black pepper to taste

Directions:

1. In a bowl, mix all ingredients except for the parmesan and whisk well. Pour this into a pan that fits your air fryer, place it in preheated fryer and cook at 350°F for 15 minutes
2. Divide the omelet between plates and serve with the parmesan sprinkled on top

Tofu and Bell Peppers

Preparation Time: 15 minutes

Servings: 8

Ingredients:

- 1 green onion; chopped.
- 3 oz. firm tofu; crumbled
- 1 orange bell pepper; cut into strips
- 1 yellow bell pepper; cut into strips
- 1 green bell pepper; cut into strips
- 2 tbsp. parsley; chopped.
- Salt and black pepper to taste

Directions:

1. In a pan that fits your air fryer, place the bell pepper strips and mix
2. Then add all remaining ingredients, toss and place the pan in the air fryer. Cook at 400 °F for 10 minutes. Divide between plates and serve

Cumin Eggplant Mix

Preparation Time: 10 minutes

Cooking time: 20 minutes

Servings: 4

Ingredients:

- 1 red onion, chopped
- 1 pound eggplant, roughly cubed
- 1 cup cherry tomatoes, halved
- Salt and black pepper to the taste
- 2 tablespoons olive oil
- ½ teaspoon chili powder
- ½ teaspoon cumin, ground
- 1 tablespoon chives, chopped

Directions:

1. Heat up the air fryer with the oil at 350 degrees F, add the eggplants and the other ingredients, toss gently, and cook for 20 minutes.
2. Divide the mix between plates and serve as a side dish.

Nutrition:

Calories 110, fat 5, fiber 3, carbs 13, protein 9

Broccoli Stew

Preparation Time: 20 minutes

Servings: 4

Ingredients:

- 1 broccoli head, florets separated
- ¾ cup tomato sauce
- ¼ cup celery; chopped.
- 3 spring onions; chopped.
- 3 tbsp. chicken stock
- Salt and black pepper to taste.

Directions:

1. In a pan that fits your air fryer, mix all the ingredients, toss, introduce the pan in your fryer and cook at 380 °F for 15 minutes
2. Divide into bowls and serve for lunch.

Nutrition:

Calories: 183; Fat: 4g; Fiber: 2g; Carbs: 4g; Protein: 7g

Cheese and Macaroni Balls

Preparation Time: 25 minutes

Servings: 2

Ingredients:

- 2 cups leftover macaroni
- 1 cup milk
- 1 cup cheddar cheese; shredded
- 3 large eggs
- 1/2 cup flour
- 1 cup breadcrumbs
- 1/2 teaspoon salt
- 1/4 teaspoon black pepper

Directions:

1. In a large bowl combine leftover macaroni and shredded cheese. Set aside.
2. In another bowl place flour; and in other - breadcrumbs. In medium bowl whisk eggs and milk.

3. Using ice-cream scoop, make balls from mac'n cheese mixture and roll them first in a flour, then in eggs mixture and then in breadcrumbs.

4. Preheat the Air Fryer to 365 - degrees Fahrenheit and cook mac'n cheese balls for about 10 minutes, stirring occasionally until cook and crispy. Serve with ketchup or another sauce.

Mozzarella Patties

Preparation Time: 25 minutes

Servings: 5

Ingredients:

- 4 large eggs
- 1-pound Mozzarella cheese
- 20 slices pepperoni

- 1 tablespoon Italian seasoning
- 1 cup all-purpose flour
- 2 cups breadcrumbs
- Salt and black pepper; to taste

Directions:

1. Slice Mozzarella cheese into 1/4-inch slices and cut each slice in half.
2. Create cheese sandwiches with Mozzarella halves and pepperoni inside. Press to seal.
3. In three different bowls place beaten eggs, breadcrumbs with Italian seasoning, and flour. Dip each cheese sandwich into flour; then into eggs and then into breadcrumb mixture.
4. Preheat the Air Fryer to 390 - degrees Fahrenheit and cook cheese patties for about 6 – 8 minutes, turning once while cooking. Serve with dipping sauce and enjoy.

Green Bean Casserole

Preparation Time: 25 minutes

Servings: 4

Ingredients:

- 1 lb. fresh green beans, edges trimmed
- ½ oz. pork rinds, finely ground
- 1 oz. full-fat cream cheese
- ½ cup heavy whipping cream.
- ¼ cup diced yellow onion
- ½ cup chopped white mushrooms
- ½ cup chicken broth
- 4 tbsp. unsalted butter.
- ¼ tsp. xanthan gum

Directions:

1. In a medium skillet over medium heat, melt the butter. Sauté the onion and mushrooms until they become soft and fragrant, about 3–5 minutes.

2. Add the heavy whipping cream, cream cheese and broth to the pan. Whisk until smooth. Bring to a boil and then reduce to a simmer. Sprinkle the xanthan gum into the pan and remove from heat
3. Chop the green beans into 2-inch pieces and place into a 4-cup round baking dish. Pour the sauce mixture over them and stir until coated. Top the dish with ground pork rinds. Place into the air fryer basket
4. Adjust the temperature to 320 Degrees F and set the timer for 15 minutes. Top will be golden and green beans fork tender when fully cooked. Serve warm.

Nutrition:

Calories: 267; Protein: 3.6g; Fiber: 3.2g; Fat: 23.4g; Carbs: 9.7g

Cabbage and Radishes Mix

Preparation Time: 20 minutes

Servings: 4

Ingredients:

- 6 radishes; sliced
- 6 cups green cabbage; shredded
- ¼ cup green onions; chopped.
- ½ cup celery leaves; chopped.
- 3 tbsp. olive oil

- 2 tbsp. balsamic vinegar
- ½ tsp. hot paprika
- 1 tsp. lemon juice

Directions:

1. In your air fryer's pan, combine all the ingredients and toss well.
2. Introduce the pan in the fryer and cook at 380 °F for 15 minutes. Divide between plates and serve as a side dish

Nutrition:

Calories: 130; Fat: 4g; Fiber: 3g; Carbs: 4g; Protein: 7g

Coriander Artichokes

Preparation Time: 20 minutes

Servings: 4

Ingredients:

- 12 oz. artichoke hearts
- 1 tsp. coriander, ground
- 1 tbsp. lemon juice
- ½ tsp. cumin seeds

- ½ tsp. olive oil
- Salt and black pepper to taste.

Directions:

1. In a pan that fits your air fryer, mix all the ingredients, toss, introduce the pan in the fryer and cook at 370 °F for 15 minutes
2. Divide the mix between plates and serve as a side dish.

Nutrition:

Calories: 200; Fat: 7g; Fiber: 2g; Carbs: 5g; Protein: 8g

Roasted Garlic

Preparation Time: 25 minutes

Servings: 12 cloves

Ingredients:

- 1 medium head garlic
- 2 tsp. avocado oil

Directions:

1. Remove any hanging excess peel from the garlic but leave the cloves covered. Cut off ¼ of the head of garlic, exposing the tips of the cloves
2. Drizzle with avocado oil. Place the garlic head into a small sheet of aluminum foil, completely enclosing it. Place it into the air fryer basket. Adjust the temperature to 400 Degrees F and set the timer for 20 minutes. If your garlic head is a bit smaller, check it after 15 minutes
3. When done, garlic should be golden brown and very soft

4. To serve, cloves should pop out and easily be spread or sliced. Store in an airtight container in the refrigerator up to 5 days.
5. You may also freeze individual cloves on a baking sheet, then store together in a freezer-safe storage bag once frozen.

Nutrition:

Calories: 11; Protein: 0.2g; Fiber: 0.1g; Fat: 0.7g; Carbs: 1.0g

Kernel and Sweet Corn Fritters

Preparation Time: 20 minutes

Servings: 4

Ingredients:

- 1 yellow onion; finely chopped
- 1 medium-sized carrot; grated
- 4 ounces canned sweet corn kernels; drained
- 1 teaspoon sea salt flakes
- 1 heaping tablespoon fresh cilantro; chopped
- 2 tablespoons plain milk

- 1 medium-sized egg; whisked
- 1 cup of Parmesan cheese; grated
- 1/4 cup of self-rising flour
- 1/3 teaspoon baking powder
- 1/3 teaspoon brown sugar

Directions:

1. Press down the grated carrot in the colander to remove excess liquid.
2. Then; spread the grated carrot between several sheets of kitchen towels and pat it dry.
3. Then; mix the carrots with the remaining ingredients in the order listed above.
4. Roll 1 tablespoon of the mixture into a ball; gently flatten it using the back of a spoon or your hand.
5. Now; repeat with the remaining ingredients.
6. Spitz the balls with a nonstick cooking oil. Cook in a single layer at 350 degrees for 8 to 11 minutes or until they're firm to touch in the center.
7. Serve warm and enjoy.

Easy Sweet Potato Curry Fries

Preparation Time: 55 minutes

Servings: 2

Ingredients:

- Pounds sweet potatoes
- 2 tablespoon olive oil
- 1 teaspoon curry powder
- salt to taste

Directions:

1. Preheat Air Fryer to 390 - degrees Fahrenheit.
2. Wash and cut sweet potatoes into fine long fries. Add oil in the pan and bake the fried for 25 minutes.
3. Now season them with curry and salt. Serve with ketchup and enjoy.

Swordfish Steaks and Tomatoes

Preparation Time: 15 minutes

Servings: 2

Ingredients:

- 2 1-inch thick swordfish steaks
- 30 oz. canned tomatoes; chopped.
- 2 tbsp. capers, drained
- 1 tbsp. red vinegar

- 2 tbsp. oregano; chopped.
- A pinch of salt and black pepper

Directions:

1. In a pan that fits the air fryer, combine all the ingredients, toss, put the pan in the fryer and cook at 390 °F for 10 minutes, flipping the fish halfway
2. Divide the mix between plates and serve

Nutrition:

Calories: 280; Fat: 12g; Fiber: 4g; Carbs: 6g; Protein: 11g

Salmon Jerky

Preparation Time: 4 hours 5 minutes

Servings: 4

Ingredients:

- 1 lb. salmon, skin and bones removed
- ½ tsp. ground ginger
- ¼ cup soy sauce
- ¼ tsp. red pepper flakes

- ½ tsp. liquid smoke
- ¼ tsp. ground black pepper
- Juice of ½ medium lime

Directions:

1. Slice salmon into ¼-inch-thick slices, 4-inch long
2. Place strips into a large storage bag or a covered bowl and add remaining ingredients. Allow marinating for 2 hours in the refrigerator
3. Place each strip into the air fryer basket in a single layer. Adjust the temperature to 140 Degrees F and set the timer for 4 hours. Cool then store in a sealed container until ready to eat.

Nutrition:

Calories: 108; Protein: 15.1g; Fiber: 0.2g; Fat: 4.1g; Carbs: 1.0g

Lime Baked Salmon

Preparation Time: 22 minutes

Servings: 2

Ingredients:

- 2: 3-oz.salmon fillets, skin removed
- ½ medium lime, juiced
- ¼ cup sliced pickled jalapeños
- 2 tbsp. chopped cilantro
- 1 tbsp. salted butter; melted.
- ½ tsp. finely minced garlic
- 1 tsp. chili powder

Directions:

1. Place salmon fillets into a 6-inch round baking pan. Brush each with butter and sprinkle with chili powder and garlic
2. Place jalapeño slices on top and around salmon. Pour half of the lime juice over the salmon and cover with foil. Place pan into the air fryer basket. Adjust the temperature to 370 Degrees

F and set the timer for 12 minutes

3. When fully cooked, salmon should flake easily with a fork and reach an internal temperature of at least 145 Degrees F.

4. To serve, spritz with remaining lime juice and garnish with cilantro.

Nutrition:

Calories: 167; Protein: 15.8g; Fiber: 0.7g; Fat: 9.9g; Carbs: 1.6g

Salmon and Jasmine Rice

Preparation Time: 35 minutes

Servings: 2

Ingredients:

- 2 wild salmon fillets; boneless
- 1/2 cup jasmine rice
- 1 tbsp. butter; melted
- 1/4 tsp. saffron
- 1 cup chicken stock
- Salt and black pepper to taste

Directions:

1. Add all ingredients except the fish to a pan that fits your air fryer; toss well
2. Place the pain in the air fryer and cook at 360 °F for 15 minutes
3. Add the fish, cover and cook at 360 °F for 12 minutes more. Divide everything between plates and serve right away.

Chicken with Pineapple

Preparation time: 10 - 20,

Cooking time: 15 – 30;

Serve: 6

Ingredients:

- 600g chicken breast
- 350 g canned pineapple
- 1 tbsp of starch
- 50 ml pineapple juice
- ½ tbsp ginger
- ½ tbsp curry
- 15 ml soy sauce
- Flour (sufficient quantity)
- Salt to taste
- Pepper to taste

Direction:

1. The floured chicken cut into small pieces, salt, and pepper in the basket previously greased.

2. Simmer for 8 minutes at 180 °C (If, at the end of cooking, the chicken pieces stick together, separate them with a wooden spoon).
3. Add the pineapple into small pieces, ginger and curry and simmer for added 3 minutes.
4. Finally, add water, soy sauce and diluted starch to pineapple juice. Simmer for another 6 minutes until the sauce has thickened.
5. Ideal accompanied with basmati rice.

Nutrition:

Calories 222, Fat 7.1g, Carbohydrates 11g, Sugars 9.7g, Protein 27g, Cholesterol 85mg

Chicken Curry

Preparation time: 10-20,

Cooking time: 15-30;

Serve: 6

Ingredients:

- 600g chicken breast
- 2 carrots
- 1 onion
- 150 ml
- 200 ml of fresh cream
- 100 ml of milk
- 2 spoons of curry
- Flour 00 (sufficient quantity)
- Salt to taste

Direction:

1. Chop the onion in a food processor and cut the carrots into cubes or slices.

2. Spray the basket and distribute the onion and carrots evenly in the basket.
3. Brown for 5 minutes at 150 °C.
4. Add the floured chicken, cut into small pieces, the broth, salt, and simmer for another 5 min.
5. Finally, pour the fresh cream, the milk and finish cooking for another 15 min. Ideally accompanied with basmati rice.

Nutrition:

Calories 243, Fat 11g, Carbohydrates 7.5g, Sugars 2g, Protein 28g, Cholesterol 74mg

Chicken and Veggies

Preparation Time: 35 minutes

Servings: 4

Ingredients:

- 4 chicken breasts; boneless and skinless
- 1 celery stalk; chopped.
- 3 garlic cloves; minced
- 1 red onion; chopped.
- 2 tbsp. olive oil
- 1 tsp. sage; dried
- 1 carrot; chopped.
- 1 cup chicken stock
- 1/2 tsp. rosemary; dried
- Salt and black pepper to taste

Directions:

1. In a pan that fits your air fryer, place all ingredients and toss well
2. Put the pan in the fryer and cook at 360°F for 25 minutes. Divide everything between plates, serve and enjoy!

Turkey Meatballs

Preparation Time: 25 minutes

Servings: 8

Ingredients:

- 1 lb. turkey meat; ground
- 1/4 cup parsley; chopped.
- 1/2 cup panko breadcrumbs
- 1/4 cup milk
- 1 tsp. fish sauce
- 1 tsp. oregano; dried
- 1 egg; whisked
- 1 yellow onion; minced
- 1/4 cup parmesan cheese; grated
- 4 garlic cloves; minced
- 2 tsp. soy sauce
- Cooking spray
- Salt and black pepper to taste

Directions:

1. In a bowl, mix together all of the ingredients: except the cooking spray), stir well and then shape into medium-sized meatballs
2. Place the meatballs in your air fryer's basket, grease them with cooking spray and cook at 380°F for 15 minutes. Serve the meatballs with a side salad

Paprika Lamb Chops

Preparation time: 10 minutes

Cooking time: 25 minutes

Servings: 4

Ingredients:
- 1 pound lamb chops
- 1 tablespoon smoked paprika
- 2 tablespoons butter, melted

- 1 garlic clove, minced
- ½ teaspoon nutmeg, ground
- ¼ cup beef stock
- Salt and black pepper to the taste

Directions:

1. In the air fryer's pan, mix the lamb chops with the melted butter and the other ingredients, toss and cook at 380 degrees F for 25 minutes.
2. Divide everything between plates and serve.

Nutrition:

Calories 310, Fat 8, Fiber 10, Carbs 19, Protein 25

Chinese Style Pork Meatballs

Preparation Time: 15 minutes

Cooking Time: 20 minutes

Servings: 3

Ingredients:
- 1 egg, beaten
- 6-ounce ground pork
- 1 teaspoon oyster sauce
- ¼ cup cornstarch

- ½ tablespoon light soy sauce
- ½ teaspoon sesame oil
- ¼ teaspoon five spice powder
- ½ tablespoon olive oil
- ¼ teaspoon brown sugar

Directions:

1. Preheat the Air fryer to 390 degrees F and grease an Air fryer basket.
2. Mix all the ingredients in a bowl except cornstarch and oil until well combined.
3. Shape the mixture into equal-sized balls and place the cornstarch in a shallow dish.
4. Roll the meatballs evenly into cornstarch mixture and arrange in the Air fryer basket.
5. Cook for about 10 minutes and dish out to serve warm.

Nutrition:

Calories: 171, Fat: 6.6g, Carbohydrates: 10.8g, Sugar: 0.7g, Protein: 16.9g, Sodium: 254mg

Italian Beef Meatballs

Preparation Time: 10 minutes

Cooking Time: 15 minutes

Servings: 6

Ingredients:

- 2 large eggs
- 2 pounds ground beef
- ¼ cup fresh parsley, chopped

- ¼ cup Parmigiano Reggiano, grated
- 1¼ cups panko breadcrumbs
- 1 teaspoon dried oregano
- 1 small garlic clove, chopped
- 1 teaspoon vegetable oil
- Salt and black pepper, to taste

Directions:

1. Preheat the Air fryer to 350 degrees F and grease an Air fryer basket.
2. Mix beef with all other ingredients in a bowl until well combined.
3. Make equal-sized balls from the mixture and arrange the balls in the Air fryer basket.
4. Cook for about 13 minutes and dish out to serve warm.

Nutrition:

Calories: 398, Fat: 13.8g, Carbohydrates: 3.6g, Sugar: 1.3g, Protein: 51.8g, Sodium: 272mg

Beef, Olives and Tomatoes

Preparation time: 10 minutes

Cooking time: 35 minutes

Servings: 4

Ingredients:

- 2 pounds beef stew meat, cubed
- 1 cup cherry tomatoes, halved
- 1 cup black olives, pitted and halved
- 1 tablespoon smoked paprika
- 3 tablespoons olive oil
- 1 teaspoon coriander, ground
- Salt and black pepper to the taste

Directions:

1. In the air fryer's pan, mix the beef with the olives and the other ingredients, toss and cook at 390 degrees F for 35 minutes.
2. Divide between plates and serve.

Nutrition:

Calories 291, Fat 12, Fiber 9, Carbs 20, Protein 26

Sage Pork

Preparation Time: 60 minutes

Servings: 6

Ingredients:

- 2½ lbs. pork loin; boneless and cubed
- 3/4 cup beef stock
- 3 tsp. sage; dried
- 1 tsp. basil; dried

- 1 tsp. oregano; dried
- 1/2 tbsp. smoked paprika
- 1/2 tbsp. garlic powder
- 2 tbsp. olive oil
- Salt and black pepper to taste

Directions:

1. In a pan that fits your air fryer, heat up the oil over medium heat.
2. Add the pork, toss and brown for 5 minutes
3. Add the paprika, sage, garlic powder, basil, oregano, salt and pepper; toss and cook for 2 more minutes.
4. Next, add the stock and toss
5. Place the pan in the fryer and cook at 360°F for 40 minutes. Divide everything between plates and serve.

Pork Sausage Casserole

Servings: 4

Preparation Time: 15 minutes

Cooking Time: 30 minutes

Ingredients

- 2 eggs
- 6 ounces flour, sifted
- 1 red onion, thinly sliced
- 1 garlic clove, minced
- ¾ cup milk
- 2/3 cup cold water
- 8 small sausages
- 8 fresh rosemary sprigs
- Salt and ground black pepper, as required

Directions:

1. In a bowl, mix together the flour, and eggs.
2. Add the onion, garlic, salt, and black pepper. Mix them well.

3. Gently, add in the milk, and water and mix until well combined.
4. In each sausage, pierce 1 rosemary sprig.
5. Set the temperature of air fryer to 320 degrees F. Grease a baking dish.
6. Arrange sausages into the prepared baking dish and top evenly with the flour mixture.
7. Air fry for about 30 minutes.
8. Remove from the air fryer and serve warm.

Nutrition:

Calories: 334, Carbohydrate: 37.7g, Protein: 14g, Fat: 14g, Sugar: 3.5g, Sodium: 250mg

Sautéed Pork with Peppers

Preparation time: 20 minutes,

Cooking time: 30 minutes;

Serve: 6

Ingredients

- 200 g of peppers
- 600 g pieces of pork taken from the loin or shoulder
- 1 shallot
- Salt to taste
- Pepper to taste

Directions:

1. Preheat the air fryer at 150 °C for 5 minutes. Spray the basket.
2. Chop the shallot and cut the peppers into strips Place the shallot and oil in the basket then brown for 2 minutes.

3. Add the peppers and simmer for another 8 minutes.

4. Finally pour the pieces of pork, salt, pepper, and simmer for another 10 minutes.

Nutrition:

Calories 334.2, Fat 11.5 g, Carbohydrate 31.8 g, Sugars 2.0 g, Protein 24.5 g, Cholesterol 59.2 mg

Spicy Tofu

Preparation Time: 10 minutes

Cooking Time: 13 minutes

Servings: 3

Ingredients:

- 1: 14-ounces block extra-firm tofu, pressed and cut into ¾-inch cubes
- 3 teaspoons cornstarch

- 1½ tablespoons avocado oil
- 1½ teaspoons paprika
- 1 teaspoon onion powder
- 1 teaspoon garlic powder
- Salt and black pepper, to taste

Directions:

1. Preheat the Air fryer to 390 degrees F and grease an Air fryer basket.
2. Mix the tofu, oil, cornstarch, and spices in a bowl and toss to coat well.
3. Arrange the tofu pieces in the Air fryer basket and cook for about 13 minutes, tossing twice in between.
4. Dish out the tofu onto serving plates and serve hot.

Nutrition:

Calories: 121, Fat: 6.6g, Carbohydrates: 7g, Sugar: 1.4g, Protein: 11.3g, Sodium: 68mg

Spicy Mushroom Soup

Preparation Time: 5 minutes

Cooking Time: 11 minutes

Servings: 2

Ingredients:

- 1 cup mushrooms, chopped
- 2 tsp. garam masala
- ½ tsp. chili powder
- 3 tbsp. olive oil
- 1 tsp. fresh lemon juice
- ¼ cup fresh celery, chopped
- 5 cups chicken stock
- 2 garlic cloves, crushed
- 1 onion, chopped
- ½ tsp. black pepper
- 1 tsp. sea salt

Directions:

1. Add oil into air fryer and set on Sauté mode.
2. Add garlic and onion to the pot. Sauté for 5 minutes.
3. Add chili powder and garam masala. Cook for a minute.
4. Add remaining ingredients and stir well.
5. Secure pot with lid and cook on manual high pressure for 5 minutes.
6. Quick release pressure then open the lid.
7. Puree the soup using a blender and serve.

Nutrition:

Calories – 244 Protein – 3.9 g. Fat – 22.8 g. Carbs – 10.2 g.

Creamy Potato Soup

Preparation Time: 5 minutes

Cooking Time: 9 minutes

Servings: 6

Ingredients:

- 3 lbs. russet potatoes, peeled and diced
- 3 cups chicken broth
- 15 oz. can coconut milk
- ½ tsp. dried thyme
- 2 carrots, peeled and sliced
- 3 garlic cloves, minced
- 1 onion, chopped
- 2 tbsp. olive oil
- Pepper
- Salt

Directions:

1. Add oil into air fryer and set on Sauté mode.
2. Add onion and garlic. Sauté for 3-4 minutes.
3. Add the rest of the ingredients except for coconut milk and stir well.
4. Secure pot with lid and cook on manual high pressure for 9 minutes.
5. Quick release pressure then open the lid.
6. Puree the soup using an immersion blender until smooth.
7. Add coconut milk and stir well.
8. Season soup with pepper and salt.
9. Serve and enjoy.

Nutrition:

Calories – 373 Protein – 20.7 g. Fat – 20.7 g. Carbs – 42.3 g.

Air fryer Fish Stew

Preparation Time: 5 minutes

Cooking Time: 15 minutes

Servings: 4

Ingredients:

- 4 tablespoons of extra-virgin olive oil
- 1 medium red onion, chopped
- 4 garlic cloves, chopped
- ½ cup of dry white wine
- 8-ounce clam juice
- 2 1/2 cups of water
- ½ pound potatoes, diced
- 1 1/2 cups of fresh tomatoes with juices
- kosher salt
- black pepper for taste
- pinch of crushed red pepper for taste
- 2 pounds sea bass cut into 2-inch pieces
- 2 tablespoons lemon juice
- 2 tablespoons of fresh dill, chopped

Directions:

1. Use saute setting on your air fryer and cook onions in 2 tablespoons of olive oil for 3 minutes, until golden brown.
2. Add the chopped garlic, saute until fragrant.
3. Add the white wine, scrape up any brown bits, until about half of the wine has evaporated.
4. Add the clam juice, water, potatoes, tomatoes, salt, pepper, and a pinch of crushed red pepper.
5. Turn the saute off, cover and seal your air fryer, and set to manual high pressure for 5 minutes.
6. After this, quick release the pressure. Open the air fryer and turn the saute setting back on. Once the soup is simmering, add the pieces of fish, and simmer for about 5 minutes, until the fish flakes apart easily.
7. Turn off saute mode, stir in lemon juice and fresh dill and remaining olive oil. Season to taste and serve.

Nutrition:

Calories – 471 Protein – 43 g. Fat – 20 g. Carbs – 24 g.

Avocado Bites

Preparation Time: 13 minutes

Servings: 4

Ingredients:

- 4 avocados, peeled, pitted and cut into wedges
- 1 ½ cups almond meal
- 1 egg; whisked

- A pinch of salt and black pepper
- Cooking spray

Directions:

1. Put the egg in a bowl and the almond meal in another.
2. Season avocado wedges with salt and pepper, coat them in egg and then in meal almond
3. Arrange the avocado bites in your air fryer's basket, grease them with cooking spray and cook at 400 °F for 8 minutes. Serve as a snack right away

Nutrition:

Calories: 200; Fat: 12g; Fiber: 3g; Carbs: 5g; Protein: 16g

Crustless Pizza

Preparation Time: 10 minutes

Servings: 1

Ingredients:

- 7 slices pepperoni
- 2 slices sugar-free bacon; cooked and crumbled
- ½ cup shredded mozzarella cheese
- ¼ cup cooked ground sausage

- 2 tbsp. low-carb, sugar-free pizza sauce, for dipping
- 1 tbsp. grated Parmesan cheese

Directions:

1. Cover the bottom of a 6-inch cake pan with mozzarella. Place pepperoni, sausage and bacon on top of cheese and sprinkle with Parmesan
2. Place pan into the air fryer basket. Adjust the temperature to 400 Degrees F and set the timer for 5 minutes.
3. Remove when cheese is bubbling and golden. Serve warm with pizza sauce for dipping.

Nutrition:

Calories: 466; Protein: 28.1g; Fiber: 0.5g; Fat: 34.0g; Carbs: 5.2g

Portabella Pizza Treat

Preparation Time: 10 minutes

Cooking Time: 6 minutes

Servings: 2

Ingredients:

- 4 pepperoni slices
- 2 Portabella caps, stemmed
- 2 tablespoons canned tomatoes with basil
- 2 tablespoons mozzarella cheese, shredded
- 2 tablespoons Parmesan cheese, grated freshly
- 2 tablespoon olive oil
- 1/8 teaspoon dried Italian seasonings
- 1 teaspoon red pepper flakes, crushed
- Salt, to taste

Directions:

1. Preheat the Air fryer to 320 degrees F and grease an Air fryer basket.
2. Drizzle olive oil on both sides of portabella cap and season salt, red pepper flakes and Italian

seasonings.

3. Top canned tomatoes on the mushrooms, followed by mozzarella cheese.
4. Place portabella caps in the Air fryer basket and cook for about 2 minutes.
5. Top with pepperoni slices and cook for about 4 minutes.
6. Sprinkle with Parmesan cheese and dish out to serve warm.

Nutrition:

Calories: 242, Fat: 21.8g, Carbohydrates: 5.8g, Sugar: 2g, Protein: 8.8g, Sodium: 350mg

Chicken Stuffed Mushrooms

Preparation Time: 10 minutes

Cooking Time: 15 minutes

Servings: 12

Ingredients:

- 12 large fresh mushrooms, stems removed
- 1 cup chicken meat, cubed
- ½ lb. imitation crabmeat, flaked
- 2 cups butter
- 2 cloves garlic, peeled and minced
- Salt and black pepper, to taste
- 1: 8 oz.package cream cheese, softened
- Crushed red pepper, to taste
- Garlic powder, to taste

Directions:

1. Preheat the Air fryer to 375 degrees F and grease an Air fryer basket.

2. Heat butter on medium heat in a nonstick skillet and add chicken.
3. Sauté for about 5 minutes and stir in the remaining ingredients except mushrooms.
4. Stuff this filling mixture in the mushroom caps and arrange in the Air fryer basket.
5. Cook for about 10 minutes and dish out to serve warm.

Nutrition:

Calories: 383, Fat: 36.3g, Carbohydrates: 4.3g, Sugar: 1.7g, Protein: 7.3g, Sodium: 444mg

Cocoa and Nuts Bombs

Preparation Time: 13 minutes

Servings: 12

Ingredients:

- 2 cups macadamia nuts; chopped.
- ¼ cup cocoa powder
- 4 tbsp. coconut oil; melted
- 1/3 cup swerve

- 1 tsp. vanilla extract

Directions:

1. Take a bowl and mix all the ingredients and whisk well.
2. Shape medium balls out of this mix, place them in your air fryer and cook at 300 °F for 8 minutes. Serve cold

Nutrition:

Calories: 120; Fat: 12g; Fiber: 1g; Carbs: 2g; Protein: 1g

Tangy Mango Slices

Preparation Time: 10 minutes

Cooking Time: 12 hours

Servings: 6

Ingredients:

- 4 mangoes, peel and cut into ¼-inch slices
- 1/4 cup fresh lemon juice
- 1 tbsp honey

Directions:

1. In a big bowl, combine together honey and lemon juice and set aside.
2. Add mango slices in lemon-honey mixture and coat well.
3. Arrange mango slices on instant vortex air fryer rack and dehydrate at 135 °F for 12 hours.

Nutrition:

Calories – 147 Protein – 1.9 g.Fat – 0.9 g.Carbs – 36.7 g.

Avocado and Raspberries Cake

Preparation Time: 40 minutes

Servings: 4

Ingredients:

- 2 avocados, peeled, pitted and mashed
- 4 oz. raspberries
- 1 cup swerve

- 1 cup almonds flour
- 4 eggs, whisked
- 4 tbsp. butter; melted
- 3 tsp. baking powder

Directions:

1. Take a bowl and mix all the ingredients, toss, pour this into a cake pan that fits the air fryer after you've lined it with parchment paper.
2. Put the pan in the fryer and cook at 340 °F for 30 minutes
3. Leave the cake to cool down, slice and serve.

Nutrition:

Calories: 193; Fat: 4g; Fiber: 2g; Carbs: 5g; Protein: 5g

Currant Pudding

Preparation Time: 25 minutes

Servings: 6

Ingredients:
- 1 cup red currants, blended
- 1 cup coconut cream
- 3 tbsp. stevia
- 1 cup black currants, blended

Directions:

1. In a bowl, combine all the ingredients and stir well.
2. Divide into ramekins, put them in the fryer and cook at 340 °F for 20 minutes
3. Serve the pudding cold.

Nutrition:

Calories: 200; Fat: 4g; Fiber: 2g; Carbs: 4g; Protein: 6g

Yummy Rice Pudding

Preparation Time: 25 minutes

Servings: 6

Ingredients:

- 7 oz. white rice
- 1 tbsp. heavy cream
- 1 tbsp. butter; melted

- 16 oz. milk
- 1/3 cup sugar
- 1 tsp. vanilla extract

Directions:

1. Place all ingredients in a pan that fits your air fryer and stir well
2. Put the pan in the fryer and cook at 360 °F for 20 minutes. Stir the pudding, divide it into bowls, refrigerate and serve cold.

Raisin Bread Pudding

Preparation Time: 27 minutes

Servings: 3

Ingredients:

- 1 egg
- 2 bread slices; cut into small cubes
- 1 cup milk
- 1 tbsp. brown sugar
- 1 tbsp. chocolate chips
- 2 tbsp. raisins, soaked in hot water for about 15 minutes
- 1 tbsp. sugar
- 1/2 tsp. ground cinnamon
- 1/4 tsp. vanilla extract

Directions:

1. In a bowl; mix well milk, egg, brown sugar, cinnamon and vanilla extract. Stir in the raisins

2. In a baking dish, spread the bread cubes and top evenly with the milk mixture. Refrigerate for about 15 to 20 minutes. Set the temperature of air fryer to 375 °F. Remove from refrigerator and sprinkle with chocolate chips and sugar on top

3. Arrange the baking dish into an air fryer basket. Air fry for about 12 minutes. Remove from the air fryer and serve warm.

Mouth-Watering Strawberry Cobbler

Servings: 4

Cooking Time: 25 minutes

Ingredients

- 1 tablespoon butter, diced
- 1 tablespoon and 2 teaspoons butter
- 1-1/2 teaspoons cornstarch
- 1/2 cup water
- 1-1/2 cups strawberries, hulled
- 1/2 cup all-purpose flour
- 1/4 cup white sugar
- 1-1/2 teaspoons white sugar
- 1/4 cup heavy whipping cream
- 3/4 teaspoon baking powder
- 1/4 teaspoon salt

Directions:

1. Lightly grease baking pan of air fryer with cooking spray. Add water, cornstarch, and sugar. Cook for 10 minutes 390 °F or until hot and thick. Add strawberries and mix well. Dot tops with 1 tbsp butter.
2. In a bowl, mix well salt, baking powder, sugar, and flour. Cut in 1 tbsp and 2 tsp butter. Mix in cream. Spoon on top of berries.
3. Cook for 15 minutes at 390 °F, until tops are lightly browned.
4. Serve and enjoy.

Nutrition:

Calories: 255; Carbs: 32.0g; Protein: 2.4g; Fat: 13.0g

Sweet Potato Pie

Servings: 6

Preparation Time: 25 minutes

Cooking Time: 60 minutes

Ingredients

- ounces sweet potato
- 1 teaspoon olive oil

- 2 large eggs
- 1: 9-inches prepared frozen pie dough, thawed
- ¼ cup heavy cream
- 2 tablespoons maple syrup
- 1 tablespoon butter, melted
- 1 tablespoon light brown sugar
- ½ teaspoon ground cinnamon
- 1/8 teaspoon ground nutmeg
- Salt, to taste
- ¾ teaspoon vanilla extract

Directions:

1. Set the temperature of air fryer to 400 degrees F.
2. Coat the sweet potato evenly with oil.
3. Arrange the sweet potato into an air fryer basket.
4. Air fry for about 30 minutes.
5. Remove from air fryer and set aside to cool completely.
6. Peel the sweet potato and mash it completely.

7. Place the pie dough onto a floured surface and cut into 8-inch pie shell.
8. Arrange the dough shell into a greased pie pan.
9. In a large bowl, add the mashed sweet potato, and remaining ingredients and mix until well combined.
10. Place sweet potato mixture evenly over the pie shell.
11. Set the temperature of air fryer to 320 degrees F.
12. Arrange the pie pan into an air fryer basket.
13. Air fry for about 30 minutes.
14. Remove from air fryer and place the pie pan onto a wire rack to cool for about 10-15 minutes before serving.
15. Serve warm.

Nutrition:

Calories: 233, Carbohydrate: 27.8g, Protein: 3.8g, Fat: 12.2g, Sugar: 16.6g, Sodium: 212mg

Milky Doughnuts

Servings: 12

Preparation Time: 15 minutes

Cooking Time: 24 minutes

Ingredients

For Doughnuts:

- 1 cup all-purpose flour
- 1 cup whole wheat flour
- 2 teaspoons baking powder
- ½ cup milk
- ¾ cup sugar
- 1 egg
- 1 tablespoon butter, softened
- 2 teaspoons vanilla extract
- Salt, to taste

For Glaze:

- 2 tablespoons icing sugar
- 2 tablespoons condensed milk
- 1 tablespoon cocoa powder

Directions:

1. In a large bowl, mix well flours, baking powder, and salt.
2. In another bowl, add the sugar and egg. Whisk until fluffy and light.
3. Add the flour mixture and stir until well combined.
4. Add the butter, milk, and vanilla extract and mix until a soft dough forms.
5. Refrigerate the dough for at least 1 hour.
6. Now, put the dough onto a lightly floured surface and roll into ½-inch thickness.
7. With a small doughnut cutter, cut 24 small doughnuts from the rolled dough.
8. Set the temperature of air fryer to 390 degrees F. Grease an air fryer basket.
9. Place doughnuts into the prepared air fryer basket in 3 batches.
10. Air fry for about 6-8 minutes.
11. Remove from air fryer and transfer the doughnuts onto a platter to cool completely.

12. In a small bowl, mix together the condensed milk and cocoa powder.
13. Spread the glaze over doughnuts and sprinkle with icing sugar.
14. Serve.

Nutrition:

Calories: 166, Carbohydrate: 33.4g, Protein: 3.9g, Fat: 2.3g, Sugar: 16.2g, Sodium: 34mg

Fruity Tacos

Servings: 2

Preparation Time: 10 minutes

Cooking Time: 5 minutes

Ingredients

- 2 soft shell tortillas
- ¼ cup blueberries

- 4 tablespoons strawberry jelly
- ¼ cup raspberries
- 2 tablespoons powdered sugar

Directions:

1. Set the temperature of air fryer to 300 degrees F. Lightly, grease an air fryer basket.
2. Arrange the tortillas onto a smooth surface.
3. Spread two tablespoons of strawberry jelly over each tortilla and top each with berries.
4. Sprinkle each with the powdered sugar.
5. Arrange tortillas into the prepared air fryer basket.
6. Air fry for about 5 minutes or until crispy.
7. Remove from the air fryer and transfer the tortillas onto a platter.
8. Serve warm.

Nutrition:

Calories: 272, Carbohydrate: 63.4g, Protein: 3.5g, Fat: 1.8g, Sugar: 34.8g, Sodium: 26mg

Notes

www.ingramcontent.com/pod-product-compliance
Lightning Source LLC
Chambersburg PA
CBHW070102120526
44589CB00033B/1484